THE BRAIN AND NERVOUS SYSTEM

Brian R. Ward

Series consultant:
Dr A. R. Maryon-Davis
MB, BChir, MSc, MRCS, MRCP

The Human Body

Franklin Watts
London New York Sydney Toronto

First published in Great Britain 1981 by
Franklin Watts Ltd
8 Cork Street
London W1

First published in the United States of America 1981
Franklin Watts Inc.
730 Fifth Avenue
New York
N.Y. 10019

UK ISBN: 0 85166 907 7
US ISBN: 0-531-04288-X
Library of Congress Catalog Card No: 80-54825

Designed by Howard Dyke

Phototypeset by Tradespools Limited, Frome, Somerset
Printed in Great Britain by E. T. Heron, London and Essex

Acknowledgment

The illustrations were prepared by: Andrew Aloof, Marion
Appleton, Nic Cudworth, The Diagram Group, Howard
Dyke, David Holmes, David Mallott, Roy Wiltshire.

Contents

Introduction	4
The brain's protective coverings	6
The spinal cord	8
The structure of the brain	10
The brain stem	12
The cerebrum	14
The cerebellum	16
The neurons	18
How messages are passed along a neuron	20
Measuring brain waves	24
Routes through the nervous system	26
The neuron network	28
Reflex action	30
The autonomic nervous system	32
The functions of the cortex	34
Where thinking takes place	36
The "logical" brain	38
The "artistic" brain	40
Learning and memory	42
Glossary	46
Index	48

Introduction

What *is* the brain? And why do we need a nervous system?

Your brain is the most important single organ in your body. It controls everything you do – your movement, your thoughts, and your memory. Often it does not act directly. Instead it may control tiny amounts of chemicals in the blood which in turn have a strong effect on another part of the body.

Although it looks quite simple, the brain is immensely complicated. It is a mass of whitish tissue, quite soft to the touch. The brain takes up about half the volume of the head. It is positioned at the top of the head, above the eyes and ears, extending lower down at the back of the head.

Almost as important as your brain is the rest of the nervous system. The **spinal cord** runs from the brain down the spine. The brain and spinal cord together make up the **central nervous system.**

Along the length of the spinal cord thread-like **nerves** branch off, dividing and connecting with almost every part of the body. Nerves carry messages from the sense organs to the brain. They also carry instructions from the brain to other parts of the body.

The brain works like a complicated but compact telephone network, with a bewildering flow of messages passing through, being sorted, and directed to their proper destination.

The brain and its spinal cord are kept in contact with every part of the body by a finely branched system of nerves through which tiny electrical signals are continually passing.

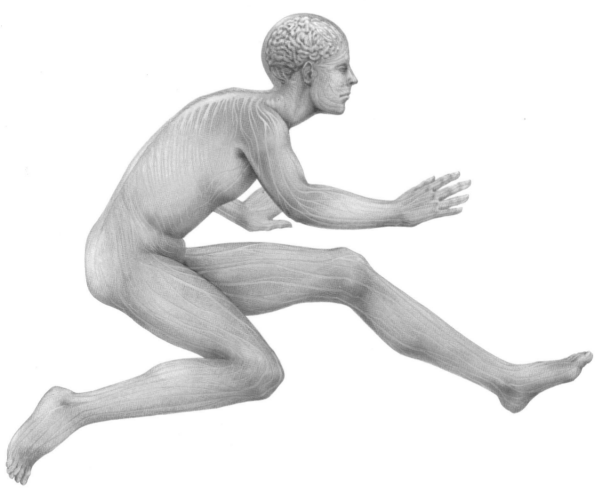

The brain's protective coverings

Because the brain is so important, it needs very good protection from accidents.

Humans stand upright, keeping the head and brain well away from bumps and knocks. Even so, much more reliable protection is needed, and the brain is protected inside the skull, which is made of tough bone.

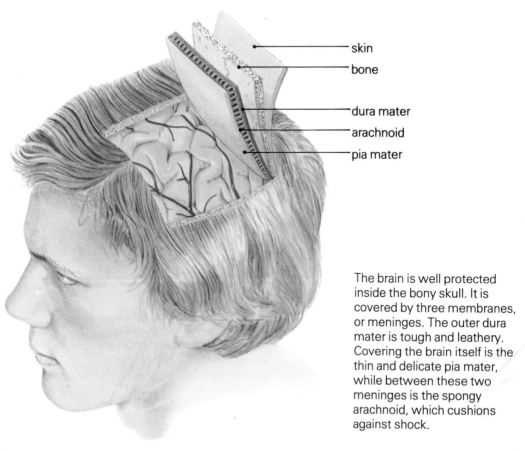

skin
bone

dura mater
arachnoid
pia mater

The brain is well protected inside the bony skull. It is covered by three membranes, or meninges. The outer dura mater is tough and leathery. Covering the brain itself is the thin and delicate pia mater, while between these two meninges is the spongy arachnoid, which cushions against shock.

Although the skull is thin, it is extremely strong because of its round shape. A rigid ball is one of the strongest shapes known. An egg, for example, is very strong, considering how thin its shell is.

So the soft and delicate brain is protected and supported by the tough skull against direct damage from outside. However even though the skull is strong and rigid, a heavy blow could still shake the brain, and cause damage. Further protection is needed, and is provided by three layers of skin-like **membranes**, called the **meninges**, which completely cover the brain. The outer membrane is called the dura mater (a Latin word, like many of the names for parts of the body). This layer is tough and leathery, and provides good protection and support.

Closest to the brain is another layer called the pia mater. It is much thinner, closely following every bump and wrinkle on the brain's surface. Between the two is the spongy arachnoid. Its spaces are filled with liquid, in which the whole brain floats, providing the final layer of protection.

There are also large spaces within the brain, and these too are filled with the same liquid, so the brain's soft tissue will not shift about as we move our heads.

The spinal cord

The spinal cord is an extension of the brain, extending about two-thirds of the way down the middle of the back to just below the ribs.

It is a rod of brain tissue, with a small hole running through it. The whole cord is covered with membranes, just like the brain, and it too is bathed inside and out with protective fluid.

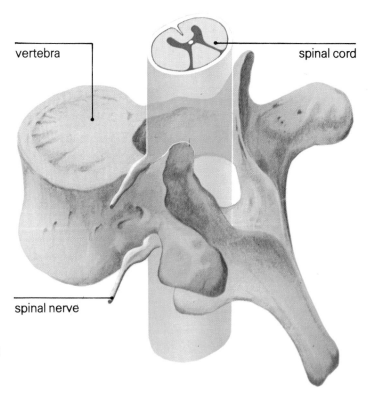

vertebra

spinal cord

spinal nerve

The delicate spinal cord is protected by the vertebrae. Each vertebra has a bony arch surrounding the spinal cord.

Like the brain, the spinal cord needs protection. While the brain is safely enclosed in a rigid skull, the spinal cord is surrounded by a set of bones called vertebrae. These make up the spinal column, which must be able to flex as we bend and turn. At the same time, the spinal column has to be strong enough to support the weight of the body, and to give very secure protection to the spinal cord.

It might seem that flexibility, strength and the protection of its fragile contents could not all be achieved by the spinal column, but its ingenious construction makes all these possible.

The spinal column is made up of more than two dozen ring-shaped vertebrae. The spinal cord runs through the hole in each vertebra, and is completely protected by an arch of bone. Bony outgrowths of the vertebrae interlock, so each vertebra can only move a small amount. This is not sufficient to pinch or damage the spinal cord.

Between each pair of vertebrae are small gaps through which nerves can pass, branching off from the spinal cord itself. The whole complicated structure is held tightly together by tough straps of ligament, and by powerful muscles.

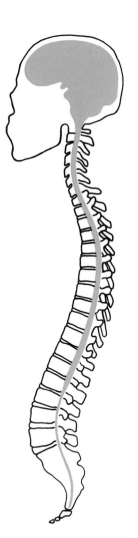

The central nervous system is made up of the brain and spinal cord, all protected within the rigid skull and flexible spine.

The structure of the brain

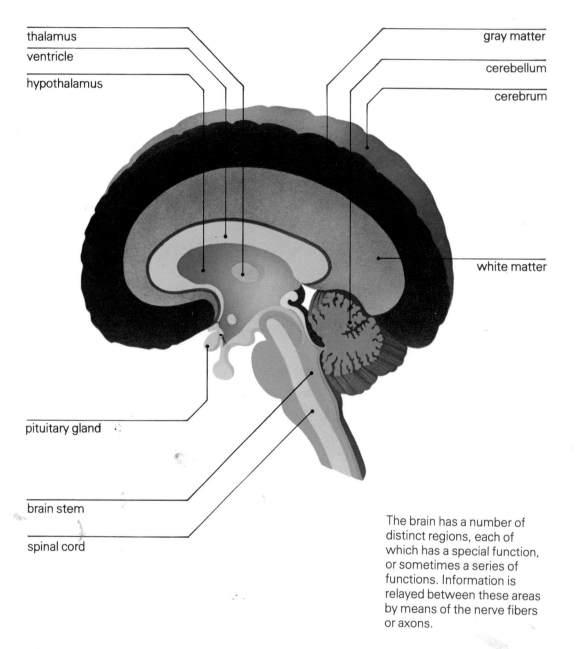

thalamus

ventricle

hypothalamus

gray matter

cerebellum

cerebrum

white matter

pituitary gland

brain stem

spinal cord

The brain has a number of distinct regions, each of which has a special function, or sometimes a series of functions. Information is relayed between these areas by means of the nerve fibers or axons.

The brain looks rather like a large pale pink walnut kernel. Its surface is deeply folded and wrinkled, and the upper part is divided almost into two by a very deep groove.

This wrinkled surface layer is the largest part of the brain, and is called the **cerebrum**. In most other animals the cerebrum is quite small, but in man it has grown so large that it covers almost all of the rest of the brain.

The cerebrum, together with other parts of the brain, grows out of the **brain stem**, which is a swelling at the top of the spinal cord.

A little further down the brain stem is the **cerebellum**, which is about one-eighth the size of the cerebrum, but outwardly similar in appearance. It is even more wrinkled, and is positioned right at the back of the head.

Several smaller parts of the brain also grow out from the brain stem – the **thalamus** and **hypothalamus**. These are completely covered by the bulk of the cerebrum.

A series of large spaces, or **ventricles**, runs through the whole brain structure, and these are filled with liquid.

The brain stem

The brain stem is sometimes called the oldest part of the brain, because it is the main part of the brain in most primitive animals. It controls most of the important functions of the body, and is our life support system. If the brain stem is not damaged, it is actually possible for the body to remain alive for some time after the rest of the brain has been destroyed in an accident.

The brain stem acts with the spinal cord to control such vital functions as the regular beating of the heart, blood pressure and breathing.

Most important of all, the brain stem controls consciousness, switching activity of the brain off as we sleep and on again as we wake. Even as we sleep, the brain stem monitors and checks our vital functions, keeping the body running smoothly.

The brain stem works like a computer, continuously checking and monitoring the information coming into the brain via the nervous system. Then it acts on this information, sending out messages into the nervous system to control the whole body. We are not aware of all this activity, although we may notice its effects. The brain stem controls functions like breathing quite automatically.

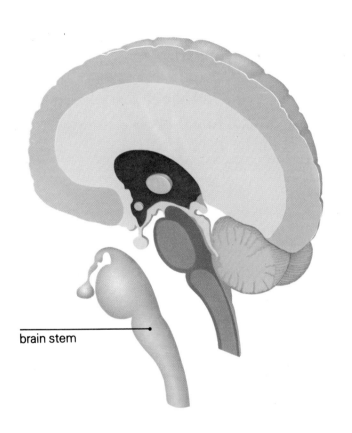

brain stem

control center

perspiration

growth

breathing

temperature

blood pressure

sleep

The brain stem, lying beneath the brain, is the body's life-support system. It works automatically, without our being aware of its function, to maintain the processes essential for life.

The cerebrum

The cerebrum is probably the youngest part of the brain, or at least the most recently developed in the course of evolution. In man it is so big that it covers almost all the rest of the brain, and makes up about seventy per cent of its whole volume.

Nerve cells are packed in the gray matter covering the cerebrum. To allow the maximum possible number of nerve cells, the cerebral surface is crumpled like a sheet of screwed-up paper.

The cerebrum consists of two large domes, or **hemispheres**, of brain tissue, joined together by a bridge called the **corpus callosum,** at the bottom of a deep cleft.

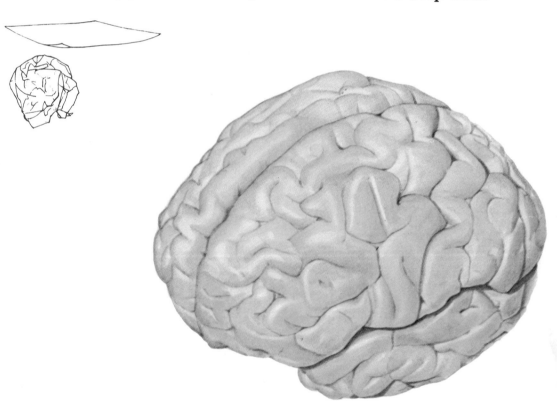

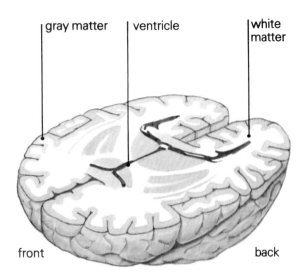

gray matter | ventricle | white matter

front | back

There are two quite different layers in the hemispheres making up the cerebrum. On the outside is a thin layer called the **cortex,** or **gray matter,** which completely covers the cerebrum. The rest of the cerebrum is made of **white matter** – the same soft tissue which makes up most of the brain.

Tiny nerve cells are closely packed in the thin layer of cortex or gray matter. The nerve fibers carrying messages down into the brain are found in the white matter. The folding of the surface of the brain means that there is more area of cortex, and therefore more brain cells can be packed in.

The cerebrum is responsible for our intelligence and for most of our skills. Here the information received from sense organs is examined and acted upon. It is the activity of our comparatively large and efficient cerebrum which makes the brain of man so much more efficient than that of other animals.

Gray matter covers the outside surface of the cerebrum. Inside, the greatest volume of the brain is made up from nerve fibers or axons, and this is called the white matter.

15

The cerebellum

cerebrum   cerebellum

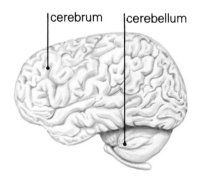

brain stem

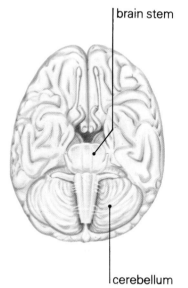

cerebellum

The cerebellum is positioned at the back of the brain, behind the cerebrum. It makes up about ten per cent of the brain's volume. Like the cerebrum, it also has an outer layer of gray matter, the rest being made up of white matter.

The inner structure of the cerebellum is quite unlike that of the rest of the brain, as the tiny cells in its cortex are arranged with almost mathematical precision. The cells are positioned in such regular order that scientists have been able to work out their connections, which resemble an enormous electrical wiring diagram.

The cerebellum works in a unique way. The rest of the brain produces signals which cause other parts of the nervous system to react. But the function of the cerebellum is to reduce or stop some of these signals, and so it controls coordination and balance.

The signals processed by the cerebellum are instructions for muscular movement that have come from the cerebrum. The signals are very strong, and if they were not adjusted in the cerebellum, we would not be able to make any accurate or delicate movements. We would be unable to pick up a glass of water without spilling it, or to walk without staggering.

16

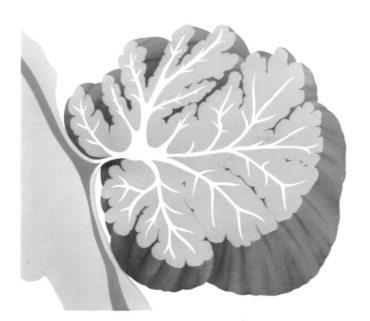

The cerebellum is a small outgrowth from the brain stem. It is very deeply folded and creased, and has a complicated but regular structure in which its neurons are arranged.

Coordination and physical skills are under the control of the cerebellum, which processes nerve impulses passing in the muscles. Without the cerebellum, the gymnast, athlete and musician would not have the fine muscular control they need.

The neurons

Nerve cells or neurons carry nerve impulses about the body. Although there are several different types, they are built on a similar plan, with a large cell body and a long axon to carry the impulse.

The tiny nerve cells that make up the brain and the rest of the nervous system are called **neurons**. There are 12 billion in the brain alone, and many million more in the nerves. Even this huge number makes up only a small part of the brain. Packed tightly around and between the neurons is another type of cell called **glial cells**. Their purpose is to provide a supporting framework for the neurons.

The neuron carries messages by means of a long strand or thread called an **axon**. The axon grows from the neuron's rounded cell body, where the other functions of the cell take place.

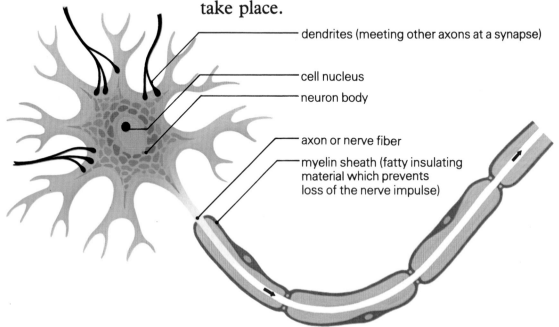

dendrites (meeting other axons at a synapse)

cell nucleus

neuron body

axon or nerve fiber

myelin sheath (fatty insulating material which prevents loss of the nerve impulse)

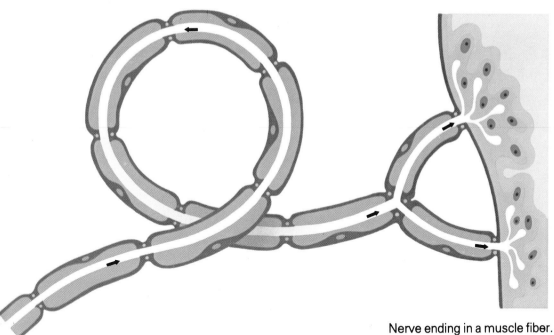

Nerve ending in a muscle fiber.
When a nerve impulse is
received here.
the muscle fiber will contract.

Many other fine threads called **dendrites**
also branch out from the neuron's cell body.
The axon is longest of all – sometimes 3 ft
(90 cm) or more in length, although the cell
body is so tiny that it can only be seen under
the most powerful microscopes. Signals are
passed along the axon, from one cell to the
next. They pass across where the branching
end of an axon meets the dendrites of
another cell, at a junction called a **synapse**.

The neuron can only pass the simplest
information – either "on" or "off." All our
mental activities are based on this simple
"on-off" signal, but when enough neurons
are involved, very complicated information
can be handled in a code rather like the
special simplified languages used to "talk"
with computers.

How messages are passed along a neuron

A signal carried by a neuron may seem like an electrical current carried along a wire, but in reality it is quite different. A tiny electrical charge *is* produced, but the movement of the signal along the axon is more like a burning gunpowder fuse. It moves along at anything between 5 and 300 ft (1·5–90 m) each second.

The axon is a thin tube filled with chemicals dissolved in water. Many are covered on the outside with a layer of fatty material, like electrical insulation.

Passing a signal along an axon involves movement of **ions**, or tiny electrically charged particles of two common metallic elements – sodium and potassium. Normally there is more potassium inside the axon and more sodium outside.

When a signal is passed, the thin skin or membrane covering the axon changes to allow the ions to leak through, causing a sudden change in the electrical properties at that point. These changes surge along the axon like a wave.

When the signal reaches the synapse, it must cross a small gap to reach the next neuron. Tiny bubbles in the knobs at the end of the axon contain chemical substances called **transmitters**. They are released as the signal reaches them, and they flow across the gap in the synapse. When they contact the dendrites of the next cell, they start the movement of sodium and potassium, passing on the signal.

Now the first neuron returns to its normal resting state, waiting for another signal.

At the synapse, or connection between two neurons, nerve impulses are carried across a tiny gap by means of chemical transmitters. These fire off another nerve impulse in the next neuron, passing on the message. In this way information is passed around the whole nervous system.

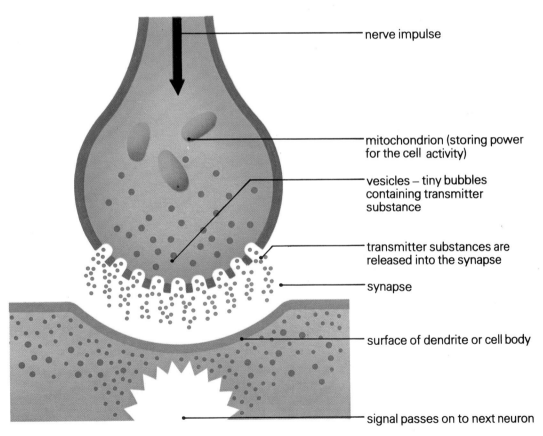

nerve impulse

mitochondrion (storing power for the cell activity)

vesicles – tiny bubbles containing transmitter substance

transmitter substances are released into the synapse

synapse

surface of dendrite or cell body

signal passes on to next neuron

The chemical transmitters which carry a signal across the gap of the synapse can be of two different types.

Some are called **excitatory chemicals**. These are the substances which pass on a message to the next neuron. This, in turn, begins the electrical changes which will cause signals to be produced and passed along its axon.

The other transmitters are called **inhibitory chemicals**. Their function is to prevent a signal being produced in another neuron.

Thousands of neurons are in contact with each other through synapses, and many will be producing excitatory or inhibitory signals. The neuron will not produce a signal unless it receives more excitatory (or "on") messages than inhibitory (or "off") messages.

A signal from one or two neurons is not enough to trigger off another – it must receive several signals at once. This means that any occasional accidental signals from the thousands of neurons around it will not cause a false message to be passed. It is rather like the principle of voting, where the neuron needs the "votes" of a number of other neurons before it is able to signal.

A nerve impulse or signal is not simply passed from one neuron to the next. It needs several nerve impulses to fire off another neuron and transmit the signal onward. As the signal is passed toward a muscle, for example, it must involve fewer and fewer neurons until, as in the drawing below, four separate signals stimulate a nerve impulse in the last neuron. This then passes its message to the muscle fiber.

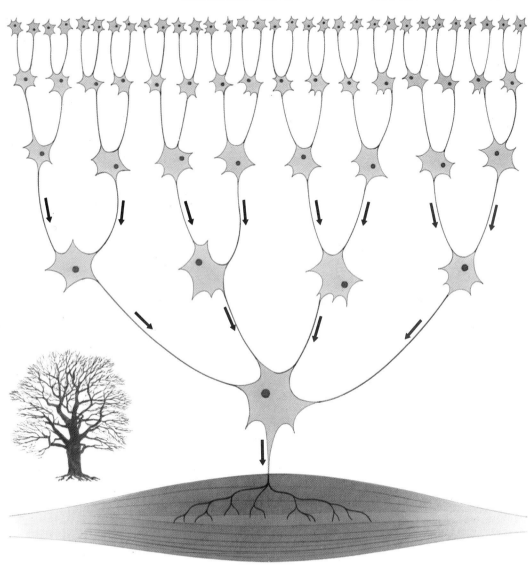

In the nervous ''tree'' fine branches join and eventually pass a signal through the ''trunk'' – a single nerve fiber.

Measuring brain waves

All over the brain, all the time, our neurons are passing their electrical signals. These flicker across the surface of the brain, spreading out like ripples from a stone dropped into a pool. If these tiny electrical signals were lights, the whole brain would twinkle endlessly, even during sleep.

Though tiny, the electrical signals from the brain can be measured, even through the skull and skin, with the aid of a special machine. Wires are stuck on to the skin, and these pick up the signals, carrying them to the machine. This records the electrical currents generated in the brain cells in graph form on a moving strip of paper. This graph is called an electroencephalogram – **EEG** for short.

An EEG shows that electrical signals are not produced steadily by the brain. Instead they come in regular short bursts. These produce a pattern on the EEG like a series of waves, sometimes called "brain waves."

The electrical activity of the brain is produced in a series of pulses which can be measured and recorded on a moving paper trace as a zigzag line. This line, or EEG, shows the amount of activity produced by the brain.

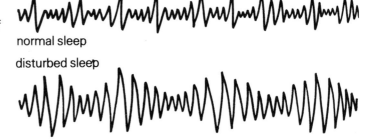

normal sleep

disturbed sleep

24

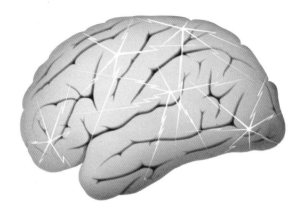

As nerve impulses pass through the brain, electrical signals spread across the surface like ripples. The brain continuously produces these electrical signals.

Brain waves show that the brain is always active, even when we sleep. The sleeping brain produces large slow waves. When we are awake, but relaxed, brain waves are faster and smaller. Activity or deep thought causes sharp jagged waves.

During brain operations it is possible to measure brain electricity much more accurately. Doctors have learned the exact function of some parts of the brain by measuring the electricity produced on its surface when, for example, a finger is pricked, or a leg is moved. The measurements have been used to produce "maps" of the cortex.

The electroencephalograph measures the electrical activity of the brain by means of sensors which are attached to the skin.

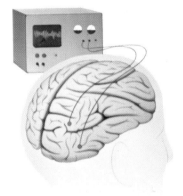

Routes through the nervous system

The electrical activity of the neurons does not take place only in the brain. From the top of the head to the tips of the toes, nerves spread through the body. They are bundles of axons, or nerve fibers, dividing and becoming finer the further away they are from the brain and spinal cord.

The neurons' cell bodies are grouped in the gray matter on the brain's surface, in similar gray matter inside the spinal cord, and in small lumps called **ganglia**, near the spine.

Through the nervous system, messages pass *to* the brain from the sense organs in the eyes, ears and mouth, as well as from the organs of touch over the whole surface of the body, and even in some internal organs. The neurons that carry these messages are called sensory neurons. More signals pass *from* the brain and spinal cord, back around the body, carried by motor neurons.

Signals pass along the whole system very quickly, but not nearly as fast as in a normal electrical circuit. It takes a certain amount of time for the signals to be carried across the synapses by the transmitter chemicals. For this reason the nerve axons are immensely long so that the messages can be carried as fast as possible without being delayed by unnecessary synapses.

The brain is involved in many of our simple daily activities. This person is testing the temperature of a bowl of water. When the foot is dipped into the water, sense organs in the skin are stimulated by the temperature and produce a signal. This is passed along nerve fibers to the brain, eventually reaching the cortex. The brain examines the incoming signals and assesses the temperature. If this is not too hot or too cold, the brain produces more signals, which pass back down the spine to leg muscles which lower the foot into the water.

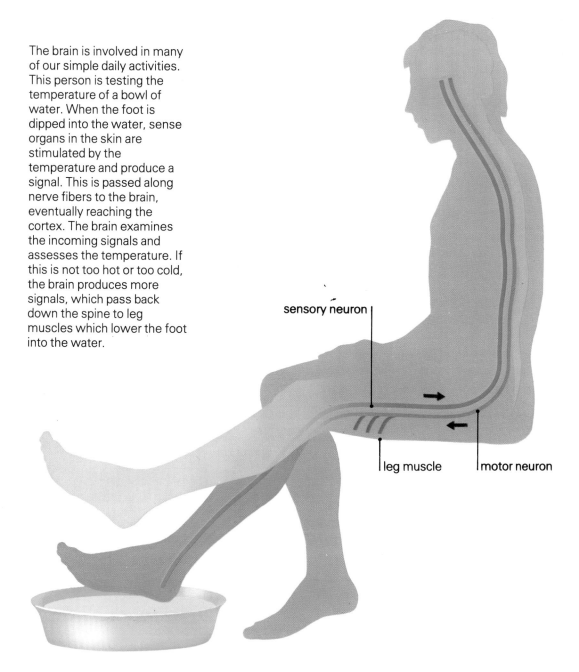

sensory neuron

leg muscle

motor neuron

The neuron network

It is difficult to realize exactly how complicated the connections of nerve cells can be. The branching ends of an axon not only touch the nearest cell, but can be in contact with another 50,000 cells or even more.

We know that messages pass from one neuron to the next in the network of cells, and a repeated signal usually always passes along the same path. If we want to say the word "brain," instructions for speech pass through the brain along a special series of pathways. If we want to say "brain" in a deeper or higher tone of voice, the muscles of the voice box must be instructed to move in another way, so the messages must move in different pathways.

The brain can select different sets of pathways to get similar results. Because of this ability, people can often overcome brain injuries, learning to use different parts of the brain to duplicate the functions of the damaged parts.

This is important to us because, unlike other body cells, brain cells cannot grow or repair themselves after we are born. Brain cells are dying every minute, but we have so many remaining to take over their function that we do not usually notice any ill effects.

Part of a circuit board used in a computer. Connections in the brain are very much more complicated, so the brain can handle more information than any machine.

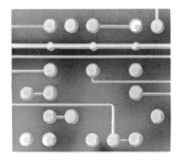

This drawing is made from an
actual photomicrograph of
part of the brain. It shows
how the neurons are arranged
in a regular manner, with
many interconnections
between nearby neurons.
There are many finer
connections, too small and
too complicated to be shown
here.

Reflex action

Control by the brain is essential for many of our functions, but in some situations it is necessary for the body to react very fast indeed, without waiting for instructions. These emergency reactions are called **reflexes.**

Jumping away from a pin-prick is a very common reaction which prevents the body from harm. It takes place very quickly, before we even recognize what has happened. This is a reflex at work.

Tiny sense organs called **receptors**, in the skin, register the pin-prick. They immediately pass signals into nerves running up the arm toward the spinal cord. The signals are then conveyed to other nerve fibers (neurons) which carry them deep into the gray matter inside the spinal cord.

When the finger is pricked, a message passes rapidly to the spinal cord. Here further impulses are generated and passed to the brain and to the muscles.

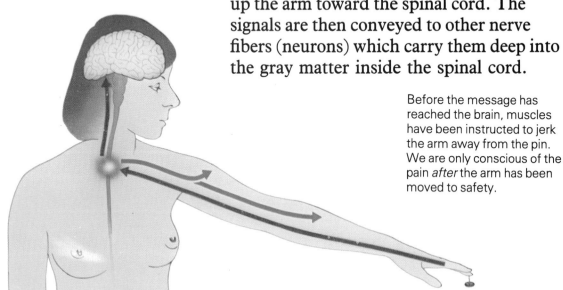

Before the message has reached the brain, muscles have been instructed to jerk the arm away from the pin. We are only conscious of the pain *after* the arm has been moved to safety.

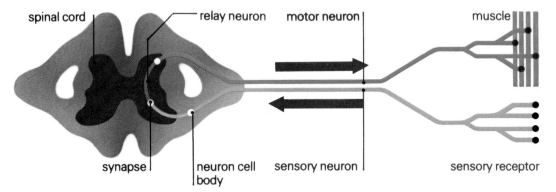

spinal cord | relay neuron | motor neuron | muscle

synapse | neuron cell body | sensory neuron | sensory receptor

Here the signals move off in two directions. Some contact nerve fibers leading directly back into the arm muscles. They cause the arm muscles to pull violently, jerking the whole arm away from the pin-prick. Part of the original signal is still speeding up the spinal cord to the brain.

A split second later we realize we have been pricked. It hurts! The brain now instructs the head and eyes to move and inspect the injury.

Sometimes we have to put up with a pin-prick, as for example when we receive a vaccination. However, we know about this in advance, and although the prick of the hypodermic needle starts the reflex, the brain has already sent an *inhibitory* message down the spinal cord. There the reflex is stopped from being completed. The arm, therefore, will not jump away.

This cross-section of the spine shows how nerve impulses enter and leave the spinal cord. In a reflex action impulses pass directly from the sensory neuron to the motor neuron, along a short relay neuron inside the spinal cord.

31

The autonomic nervous system

Some of the activities of the nervous system, like thinking and the control of movement, are very obvious to us. But the nervous system is also working without our realizing it, controlling our internal organs.

This is the responsibility of a special part of the nervous system called the **autonomic nervous system**. It regulates our blood circulation, digestion, breathing, reproductive organs and the elimination of waste from the body. It also controls important glands which have a powerful effect on the body. The autonomic nervous system works independently of most of the brain and its cell bodies are grouped in ganglia near the spine. It operates entirely by reflexes, and although the brain stem is also involved in its activity, we are not consciously aware of this.

The system is actually split into two parts, called the **sympathetic** and **parasympathetic nervous systems**. They work against each other. One system will stimulate an organ, such as a gland, making it work harder. The other system stops it from working. First one takes over, then the other, and the result is that the organ is kept working at just the right level.

The sympathetic nervous system can be

seen working when we are angry or frightened. Its action makes the heart beat faster and lets us breathe more deeply. The pupils of the eye become larger, and we go pale as blood drains from the skin to feed muscles we might need for "fight or flight." This has all happened because the sympathetic system has taken over, to make the body ready for an emergency.

Most of our normal body functions are controlled by the parasympathetic nervous system. When we are angry or excited, the sympathetic nervous system takes over, increasing the rate at which the heart beats, and making us breathe deeply to take in more oxygen.

The functions of the cortex

Different areas of the brain are responsible for registering the sense of touch, and for controlling body movement. The position of these areas can be "mapped" on the surface of the cortex.

Muscles in our internal organs work automatically, but most of our muscles work only when we wish to move them. These are voluntary muscles.

Voluntary movements, such as walking, moving the arms, and using the fingers, are directly controlled by the brain. A narrow strip of cortex across the top of the cerebrum is called the **motor cortex**, and it is concerned with organizing our movement.

The motor cortex collects information from other parts of the brain, including signals from sense organs. When a decision

The motor cortex
The areas of the cortex used to control movement are similar to those registering the senses, with the face and hands being especially important.

swallowing

tongue,jaw

lips

face
eye, brow

neck

fingers, hand

wrist

shoulder,arm

trunk

hip,knee

ankle

toes

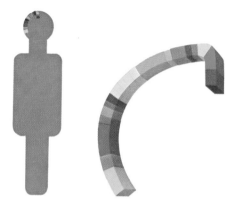

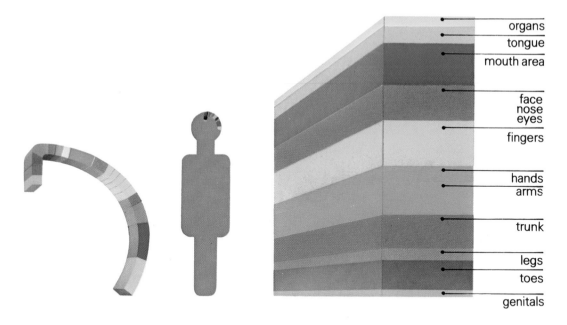

has been made to move a muscle, or a whole series of muscles, it issues its instructions to the proper part of the body.

Different parts of the motor cortex have special functions, each controlling movement in a certain part of the body. Important and complex parts, such as the hands and lips, require very careful control, and the many neurons needed for this work take up large areas of the cortex. Less complicated parts need less control, so smaller areas of the cortex are responsible for them.

In the same way that movement is controlled by the motor cortex, special parts of the **sensory cortex** are responsible for touch. Other parts look after vision, hearing, and all our other senses.

The sensory cortex
The relative importance of different senses can be seen by measuring the area they take up on the surface of the cortex. The large area taken up by hands, face and eyes can be clearly seen.

35

Where thinking takes place

Movement and the senses take up only two narrow strips across the cortex of the cerebrum.

The rest of the cortex does not have such easily recognized purposes. It contains the association areas, and is probably the part of the brain where "thinking" takes place. By thinking, we mean examining and interpreting the huge number of signals coming into the brain, and deciding on any action to take – or sometimes deciding *not* to act.

Some functions, among them speech, are dotted about the cortex in small patches. Speech is also controlled by several different areas of the brain, as well as by a part of the cortex.

The way the association areas work is not well understood. Sometimes quite large parts of the brain can be damaged, by disease or injury, without having much effect. On the other hand, damage to small parts of the brain can sometimes have very serious effect. The way the brain works is much more complicated than it at first appears.

Very large parts of the brain have no obvious purpose at all, but as the neurons are interconnected in such a complicated way, it is believed that all of the brain must have some function. Perhaps some of this "spare" brain comes into use to replace neurons that die as we get older.

As we view objects, images formed on the retina of the eye produce nerve impulses. These are carried to the brain, eventually arriving at the visual cortex, a narrow band across the cerebrum. Some of this information passes to the association areas of the cortex, where a choice is made. In this picture the boy is choosing between two drinks. The motor area of the cortex then produces signals which are sent to the arm and hand muscles, to cause the desired action.

The "logical" brain

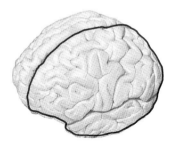

The cerebrum is divided almost into two sections by a deep groove. In some serious brain operations it has been necessary to divide them completely. When this was done, surgeons found that each half could work on its own, as a separate "brain," but the right and left sections are very different in the way they work.

Each side of the brain controls the *opposite* side of the body, nerve fibers crossing over in the corpus callosum at the bottom of the groove between the hemispheres.

Normally both sides of the brain must work together, and they communicate with each other through the corpus callosum. When this is cut, and the two sections are kept apart, the differences between them can be seen.

In most people the left side of the brain is responsible for "logical" thinking. This is the careful, step-by-step reasoning which we need for say, mathematics. We also use the left side to control our speech, an immensely complicated process which no machine has been able to master. Separate small pieces of the left cerebrum look after the actions needed for writing, for the sounds we produce as we speak, and for the naming of things we can see.

Sometimes an old person has a stroke, which damages this part of the brain, and he or she may then not be able to speak properly.

The left side of the brain works in this way in most people, but in left-handed people the right side of the brain may be the "logical" half. In some left-handed people speech may be controlled by *both* sides.

The left side of the brain is where logical or calculatory thinking takes place. While working out a problem such as arithmetic or a chess game, the left side of the brain is intensely active.

The "artistic" brain

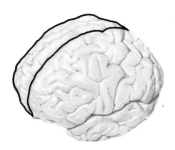

The right side of the brain is the "artistic" part. It is concerned with understanding and interpreting the world about us – but not usually with speech.

The right side of the brain looks at situations and problems in general, and gives us an immediate answer or a solution. This is quite different from the way the left side works, in a series of deliberate, careful steps.

The "artistic" brain is concerned with looking at our surroundings. It can, for example, pick out a familiar face from a crowd of people, but the left side of the brain then has to supply that person's name from the memory.

Musical abilities also depend on the right side of the brain, together with visual skills such as painting.

Although each half of the brain can operate on its own, both sections must work together if we are to function normally. For most activities we use both sides together. Imagine that you are writing a description of a picture. First you look at the picture, and the right side of your brain becomes active. A scientist could prove this by using an EEG. Now you start to write, and the left side of the brain takes over. When you look at a complicated diagram, both the "logical" and "artistic" parts of the brain are needed. Both sides work smoothly together.

The right side of the brain is used for "creative" thinking, often involving a visual problem or puzzle. The right side of the brain is skillful in recognizing shapes and patterns.

Learning and memory

The picture on the left shows part of the brain of a child of 3 months. The picture on the right shows the same part of the brain at 24 months. In the immature brain there are not many connections between the neurons. As the brain develops, and we add experiences to our memory store, the connections between the neurons become much more complicated.

Learning means making a tiny change in the structure of the brain. Signals find their way through the network of neurons in the brain, and repeated signals tend to take the same pathway each time. These pathways are made between neurons by way of synapses.

If we were to begin some new activity, such as learning to play a guitar, signals would have to be transmitted through already existing pathways to give the proper

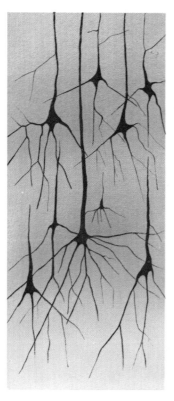
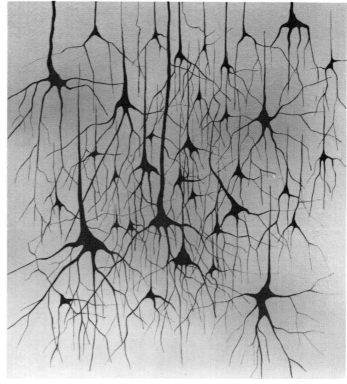

instruction to the fingers to press the guitar strings in a particular way. Since there are at first only a few pathways to choose from, the finger movements would be rather clumsy.

With more practice, the same message is passed more and more often, and the pathways begin to change. More synapses develop for the instructions to the finger muscles. As these new pathways develop, we find it much easier to move the fingers exactly as required, and eventually can play well without even looking at what we are doing. A whole section of brain has been "rewired" to act as a music-playing computer.

The brain of a young baby has far fewer connections between its neurons than an adult. These connections increase very quickly as the baby learns about its surroundings. This is why it is important to talk to very young babies and give them plenty of toys to catch their interest while their brains develop more fully.

Learning and memory are similar, and both probably depend on alterations in the brain. Memory is not well understood, but it may also depend on changes in the pathways taken through the brain by signals produced by neurons. Some scientists also think that special chemicals may be involved in storing memories. Memory is not based on any special part of the brain, but is stored over large parts of its surface.

There are several different types of memory. One is very short, and consists of a quick scan through all the material received from the sense organs. Nearly all is quickly forgotten. Sometimes something crops up which interests us, so we think about it for a while. It too will disappear within a few seconds, unless we repeat it to ourselves several times, or "rehearse" it. This seems to make the memory "stick" in the mind. It is what we have to do to remember a telephone number. After we have rehearsed it several times, or have used the number frequently, it becomes a permanent memory.

Once something is filed away in our memory, it is there for good. We sometimes "forget" something, but what really happens is that we forget how to find it in the vast storage system of the brain. Probably the proper pathway is no longer effective, because it has not been used enough. The fact we are seeking remains filed away until we can get at it along another pathway through the brain. It can also be truly lost in old age if enough brain cells die so that the storage area no longer works.

Information stored in our memory is sometimes easily accessible, but can be "mislaid" in the whole enormous filing system. There is always a large amount of unused storage space in the memory.

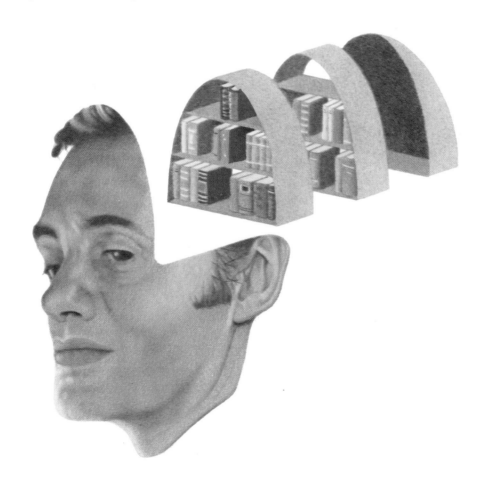

45

Glossary

Autonomic nervous system: the part of the nervous system which functions without our conscious awareness. It controls all of the life-support systems of the body.

Axon: long thread, extending from the body of a neuron, along which a signal is carried.

Brain stem: bulge at the top of the spinal cord, forming the bottom part of the brain. The brain stem controls most of our vital functions, and is a major part of the autonomic nervous system.

Central nervous system: the brain and spinal cord are the most essential parts of the nervous system, together making up the central nervous system.

Cerebellum: small and deeply folded area at the back of the brain, concerned with controlling coordination of movement and balance.

Cerebrum: large domed area making up the largest part of the brain. Our reasoning, memory and senses are controlled in the cerebrum.

Corpus callosum: small strip of tissue connecting the two hemispheres of the cerebrum. Signals passed between the right and left hemispheres cross the corpus callosum.

Cortex: the outer layer of the cerebrum, made up from gray matter.

Dendrites: the finely branched endings of an axon, which are in contact with another neuron at the synapse.

EEG: electroencephalogram; a measurement of the electrical activity within the brain, recorded as a graph on a strip of moving paper.

Excitatory chemicals: transmitter substances, present in tiny amounts, which stimulate a neuron to produce a signal.

Ganglia: small groups of neurons, in which nerve signals are processed.

Glial cells: special cells which are packed around and between the neurons. They help support the delicate nervous tissue.

Gray matter: part of the nerve tissue in which the bodies of the neurons are situated. Mostly on the *outside* of the brain, and the *inside* of the spinal cord.

Hemispheres: the two dome-like structures which make up most of the cerebrum.

Hypothalamus: small part of the brain which is concerned with expressing emotion (such as changes in pulse rate, sweating, etc.), controlling sleep, and governing the action of the most important gland in the body, the pituitary.

Inhibitory chemicals: transmitter substances which prevent the production of a signal in a neuron.

Ion: an electrically charged chemical particle. When common salt, or sodium chloride, is dissolved in water, it splits into two separate ions: sodium and chloride.

Membrane: a thin covering to a cell or tissue. Neurons are covered by a very thin membrane, through which transmitter chemicals pass.

Meninges: skin-like coverings over the brain and part of the spinal cord. There are three layers: the dura mater, arachnoid and pia mater.

Motor cortex: part of the surface of the cerebrum in which instructions for muscle movement are processed.

Nerve: bundle of axons, through which signals are passed to and from the brain.

Neuron: nerve cell, which passes signals to other neurons along a thread-like axon.

Parasympathetic nervous system: part of the autonomic nervous system which influences the pupil of the eye, pulse rate, breathing, the digestion, and sexual organs. Its action is, in general, opposite to that of the sympathetic nervous system.

Receptors: groups of cells which can receive a signal, and pass it on to the nervous system. Typical receptors are those registering touch, in the skin, and light, in the retina of the eye.

Reflex: an automatic response of the body, which initially does not involve the brain. An example of a reflex is jerking the hand away from a hot object.

Sensory cortex: part of the surface of the cerebrum in which information from the sense organs is processed and converted into the "sensations" that we feel.

Spinal cord: very large bundle of nerve cells running down from the brain inside the spine.

Sympathetic nervous system: part of the autonomic nervous system influencing pulse rate, breathing, and many other functions. Its actions are generally opposite to those of the parasympathetic nervous system, preparing the body for action in an emergency. It also controls speech and swallowing.

Synapse: the gap between a neuron and the dendrites of another neuron.

Thalamus: part of the brain which processes information from the sense organs, and provides some control over muscle activity.

Transmitter substances: chemicals present in tiny amounts, which carry a signal across a synapse, between the neurons.

Ventricles: fluid-filled spaces inside the brain, also running down the middle of the spinal cord.

White matter: masses of closely packed axons. White matter makes up most of the *interior* of the brain, and the *outside* of the spinal cord.

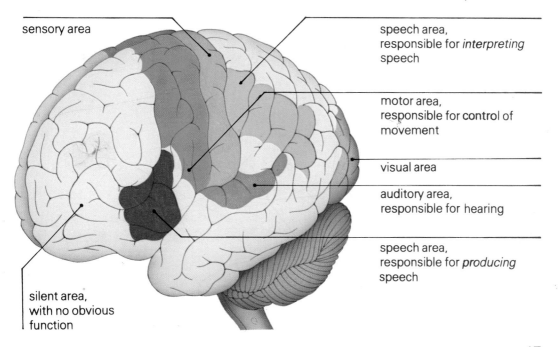

sensory area

speech area, responsible for *interpreting* speech

motor area, responsible for **control** of movement

visual area

auditory area, responsible for hearing

speech area, responsible for *producing* speech

silent area, with no obvious function

Index

arachnoid 6, 7
artistic ability 40
autonomic nervous system 32–3, 46
axon 10, 18, 19, 20, 22, 26, 28, 46

blood circulation 32
blood pressure 12
brain cells 15, 28, 45
brain damage 12, 28, 36, 38
brain stem 10, 11, 12–13, 32, 46
brain waves 24, 25
breathing 12, 32, 33

central nervous system 4, 9, 46
cerebellum 10, 11, 16–17, 46
cerebrum 10, 11, 14–15, 16, 34, 36, 38, 46
consciousness 12, 13
coordination 16, 17
corpus callosum 14, 15, 38, 46
cortex 15, 16, 25, 27, 34, 36, 46

dendrites 19, 21, 46
digestion 32
dura mater 6, 7

EEG 24, 25, 41, 46
electrical activity of brain 5, 20, 22, 24–5
excitatory chemicals 22, 46

ganglia 26, 32, 46
glial cells 18, 46
gray matter 14, 15, 16, 26, 46

hearing 35

heart beat 12, 33
hemisphere 14, 15, 38, 46
hypothalamus 10, 11, 46

inhibitory chemicals 22, 31, 46
intelligence 15
internal organs 32, 34
ions 20, 46

learning 42–3, 44
left-handedness 39
ligament 9

membrane 6, 7, 8, 20, 46
memory 4, 44–5
meninges 6, 7, 46
motor cortex 34, 35, 46
motor neuron 26, 31
movement 4, 32, 34, 35
muscles 9, 16, 23, 27, 34, 35
musical ability 40
myelin sheath 18

nerve 4, 5, 9, 26, 30, 46
nerve cell 14, 15, 18, 28
nerve fiber 10, 15, 26, 27, 30, 31, 38
neuron 17, 18, 19, 20, 21, 22, 24, 26, 29, 30, 35, 37, 42, 43, 46

parasympathetic nervous system 32–3, 46
pia mater 6, 7

receptors 30, 47
reflex 30–1, 32, 47
relay neuron 31

sense organs 4, 15, 26, 27, 34, 44

sensory cortex 35, 47
sensory neuron 26, 31
skull 6, 7, 8, 9
sleep 12, 25
speech 36, 38
spinal cord 4, 5, 8, 9, 10, 11, 26, 30, 31, 47
spine 9, 31
sympathetic nervous system 32–3, 47
synapse 19, 20, 21, 22, 26, 42, 43

thalamus 10, 11, 47
thinking 36
transmitter substances 20, 21, 22, 26, 47

ventricles 10, 11, 47
vertebrae 8, 9
vision 35, 37
visual skills 40

white matter 15, 16, 47